CREATURE COMFO

PUNCH
in the Animal Kingdom

Edited by William Hewison

A PUNCH BOOK

Published in association with

GRAFTON BOOKS

A Division of the Collins Publishing Group

LONDON GLASGOW
TORONTO SYDNEY AUCKLAND

Grafton Books
A Division of the Collins Publishing Group
8 Grafton Street, London W1X 3LA

Published by Grafton Books 1989

British Library Cataloguing in Publication Data

Creature comforts: Punch in the animal kingdom.
1. English humorous cartoons. Special subjects:
Animals – Collections
I. Hewison, William II. Punch
741.5'942

ISBN 0-246-13580-8

Printed in Great Britain by
William Collins Sons Ltd, Glasgow

Introduction

It's a mystery. I have scrutinised it from all angles, I have probed and analysed, I have drifted off into reverie in the hope that a sudden spark of inspiration will reveal the answer. But, nothing. Perhaps one of those earnest American academics with a fat Ford Foundation grant tucked in his back pocket will come to the rescue and spend some real time on the matter. I wish he would.

Because I cannot for the life of me understand how (a) the Hedgehog and (b) the Lemming have each become such a stock character in the world of cartooning. It would seem that every apprentice cartoonist is required to produce a couple of gags on each of these animals as part of his training, and thereafter knock out (an apt phrase) more of them at frequent intervals throughout his career.

How, and why, should they do it? After all, hedgehogs do nothing else but get flattened by motorists on country roads, and as for lemmings their sole activity is to gang together and chuck themselves off cliffs. Not much grist for the old cartoon-producing mill there, one would have thought, but we'd be wrong – those squashed hedgehogs and hurtling lemmings are hardly ever off the printed pages. And just when you reckon that it can't be possible to squeeze a further variation on the squashing and the jumping, some comical fellow trots in with yet another.

It's not that these cartoonists are bereft of other animal material to turn to their own account – dammit, the world is chock-a-block with the stuff. Fortunately the cartoonists are well aware of this fact, so every now and again they unhitch themselves from the lemmings and the hedgehogs and safari off into the vast territory of the animal kingdom, discovering joke material everywhere, even in the most unlikely places. Banx, for instance, coming across a Giant Panda, can imagine the surreal possibility of it tackling a free-fall parachute descent – but without a parachute – to enable it to remark, 'It's no wonder that we are an endangered species, really.' Elsewhere in these pages, Thelwell, visiting the dozy lions of Longleat, can register that Kilroy evidently got there before him.

Other comic artists collected here have bent their minds towards the longevity of turtles and the fact that crocodiles often turn up later in the shape of ladies' handbags. More popular are those St Bernard dogs lugging barrels of brandy around the countryside, rats putting in their stint for science, sloths being slothful, foxes being foxy, and, grabbing the whole bang lot at one go, Noah navigating his Ark. Otherwise, not many animal species escape the jokey treatment; even the Gnu, whose natural habitat is the page with the crossword puzzle on it, is not overlooked. And it's hardly surprising that cartoonists have gone time and time again to the multifarious activities of the domestic dog (no lemming he); after all, if you trip over the resident pooch every day he's bound to keep insinuating himself into the picture. (For acute observation of dog behaviour and stance, seek out Nick's drawing of the dog lying on the electric chair.)

So there's a substantial ration of dogs here but, curiously, there are hardly any cats; cartoonists, it would seem, are not 'cat people'. Mind, David Myers offers a beauty: a vet confronts a cat's owner with a card bearing the words, 'Has he always had such a deafening purr?'

You will notice, incidentally, that I have restricted the appearance of those lemmings and hedgehogs to a reasonable minimum.

William Hewison
March 1989

"The dog's being impossible again."

"Leave me if you must, Marjorie, but to run away with my best friend, that's what really hurts."

"Now that you've finally arrived, there's a small matter of £38.70."

"Remember, this is an important interview – I'll do the talking."

"*What's amazing is no two cats or dogs are alike!*"

"You know what I like about you? You don't
talk, talk, talk, talk, talk, talk, talk."

*"In the rush to get away, we almost forgot to leave you his
diarrhoea mixture, deodorant dust and flea powder."*

*"What worries me is who's going to conserve us if **they** become extinct?"*

"There is a queue, you know."

"If that's what we're evolving into, I give up."

ffolkes

"My goodness, Animal Lib!"

"So much for getting the bull on board."

"It's our annual parade to commemorate the Great Flood!"

"Same here – if I stay inside, the noise drives me up the wall."

"It's infuriating. Aerodynamically speaking, we're capable of two hundred miles per hour."

*"We had to introduce
rugby league every
fortnight!"*

*"Oh dear, not the **Irish** Christians again!"*

"It certainly beats pacing up and down."

"I only wounded him but then my elephant trampled him to death."

"Thank goodness! Extinct just in the nick of time!"

*"That makes it twenty-three known
surviving examples."*

"You know, out of all the animal species, I reckon the human must be about the nearest to us in intelligence."

"…Yes, but where are we all going to?"

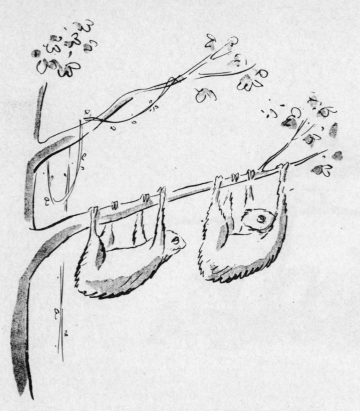

"I say the race is to the swift, and I say to hell with it!"

"There's only one thing to know about being a dormouse. Everything eats a dormouse."

"Oh, hell! Are you sure? I was hoping we were Lust."

"Sorry, I was just trying to get past."

"I thought you were supposed to be cutting out Afters."

"I don't like the look of this!"

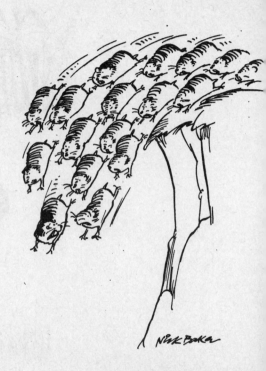

"Last time we did this I damn
nearly killed myself."

"Excuse me but I think you ought to know – you're being eaten."

"We made it! We made it! We're on the Endangered Species list!"

*"I do hope the World Wildlife Fund saves the turtle from extinction –
I'd miss turtle soup terribly."*

"It's at about seventy I get this funny knocking noise."

"We never catch the visitors at it, M'Lord."

*"I'm glad to see every animal is kept in its
natural habitat."*

*"As you can see, some have adapted to their
reduction of territory quite well."*

"Run up your clock, lady?"

"...and we use these to test metal fatigue."

"My God, they've become piper resistant!"

"Naturally, when I volunteered to become a guinea-pig, it never occurred to me..."

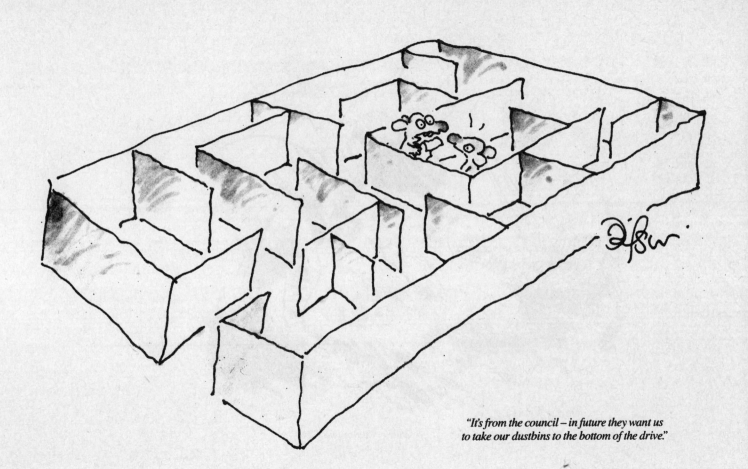

"It's from the council – in future they want us to take our dustbins to the bottom of the drive."

"...but you can call me Rex."

"Here...isn't that our babysitter?"

"*I don't think they are ready for the Wheel yet.*"

"...98...99...100...Ready or not, here come the lions and tigers!"

"How was the holiday?"

"To hell with natural selection – let's just eat the nice fat young ones."

"One of those new independent countries, I suppose."

"It's no wonder we're an endangered species, really."

"*Gentlemen! Let us prepare to enter the main burial chamber and discover riches beyond our wildest dreams.*"

"There's a furry thing in here eating cheese. I understand that's your department."

"My God! Gramophone-sniffing!"

McLACHLAN

"You spoil that cat."

"The lambs seem very subdued this year."

"You're in luck, sir – you're going in the wrong direction."

*"Pigswill, yes, but **great** pigswill!"*

"Those were the days – 'Here a cluck. There a cluck. Everywhere a cluck-cluck'."

"You know the rules – no helping the dogs."

"Did you order an economical, pollution-free, self-propelling lawnmower?"

"...*for services to Literature.*"

"I'm enrolled at the Kennel-Club – whatever a kennel is …"

"It has reached our ears …"

"It's The Wild again."

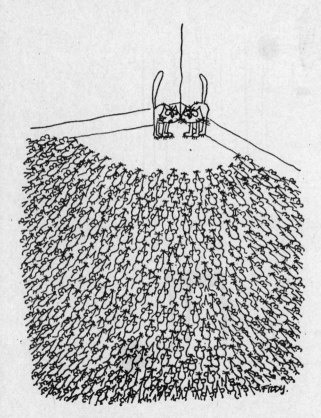

"Well don't just stand there – negotiate!"

"My goodness, getting mad won't help."

*"Well, dialect jokes, mainly – corgis,
alsatians, beagles…"*

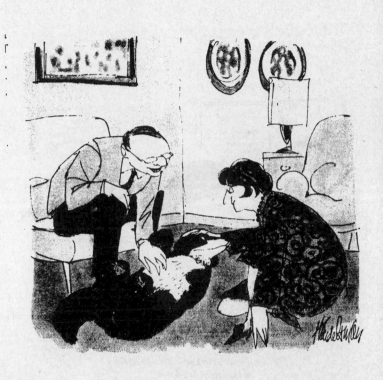

*"You've certainly held this marriage
together, haven't you, boy?"*

*"Your wife wants to know if you'll agree
to have him put down."*

"McGinty must be near . . . that one's really fresh."

"Yes sir, I just took a fox
to the fifth floor!"

"We're having trouble with foxes."

NSPCC

mike Williams.

"Nothing to it. Just keep showing them how, then, one day **you** throw the stick."

"Your weight is eight stone seven
pounds, you are faithful, stout-hearted
and extremely good with children."

*"Oh no, they're not that unusual, you're probably
thinking of the white ones."*

"Well, I've had it fifteen years, and frankly I don't reckon it as much of an aphrodisiac."

"An old friend of yours has dropped by to cheer you up."

"It's to the Unknown Regimental Mascot."

"…*and try not to lope.*"

BANX

*"I always say if you're going
to be Haute Cuisine, at
least act like Haute Cuisine."*

"What immortal hand or eye could frame thy fearful symmetry, baby?"

"Me – agnostic!"

"I'll be glad when we've crossed the bloody Equator!"

"Personally, I don't think she's seaworthy."

"Blast! – there's always trouble in the stands when Celtic are playing."

"There's a lot to be said for those convenience foods."

"Big hairy thing with horns overboard!"

"My God! This could be it."

"In this dream I was a handbag and bit the Queen Mother."

"I'd love to, dearest, but it's the noise ... I can't bear the appalling noise."

"How's the old arthritis today?"

"It's the bloody dawn chorus I can't stand."

"I do believe you're right – it is a cuckoo."

*"I was wondering if you had a piece of hooked wire or
something – I seem to have locked myself out."*

"Do you realise that in the event of a nuclear war we've got just four minutes to withdraw into our shells?"

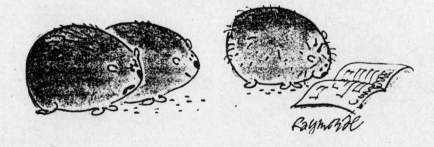

*"I'd just like to know what sort of lemming it is that gets
congratulatory telegrams from the Queen."*

"You call that music? Don't you know any Gershwin tunes?"

"If there's one thing I can't stand,
it's doing children's shows."

"You've got to hand it to him – not many people get a Sellotape-dispenser research grant."

*"I'm worried about pollution –
they might do something
about it."*

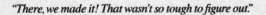

"There, we made it! That wasn't so tough to figure out."

"It beats the hell out of mazes – you just make each side a different colour, and they throw you a piece of cheese."

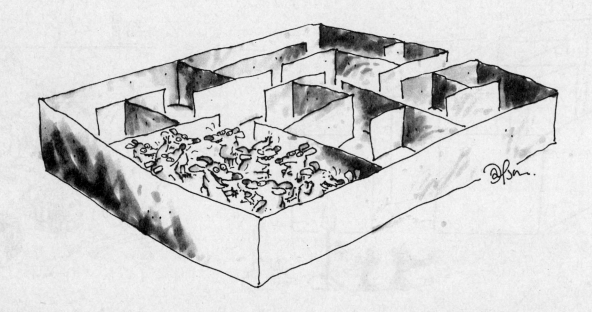

"The best parties always end up in the kitchen."

"...then along comes the mouse..."

"Hold back, Rusty – it's too obvious.
It could be a trap."

"No matter how much he begs, don't lend him any money."

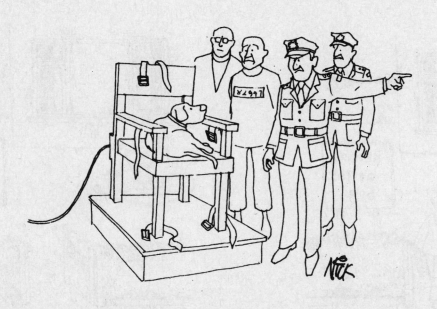

"I say, I hope that's a Dalmatian you've got there?"

"Frankly, I feel he over-disciplines his animals."

"Keeping a friendship in constant repair cuts both ways, you know."

"This is the dog that bit the cat that killed the rat that ate the malt that came from the grain that Jack sprayed."

"I can fix up your phonograph in a couple of days but we're having a hell of a job getting hold of the dogs right now."

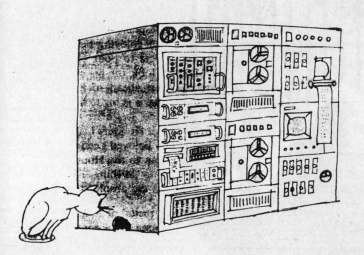

"Time was when they too had servants to open and close their doors,
clean their homes, bring them their food."

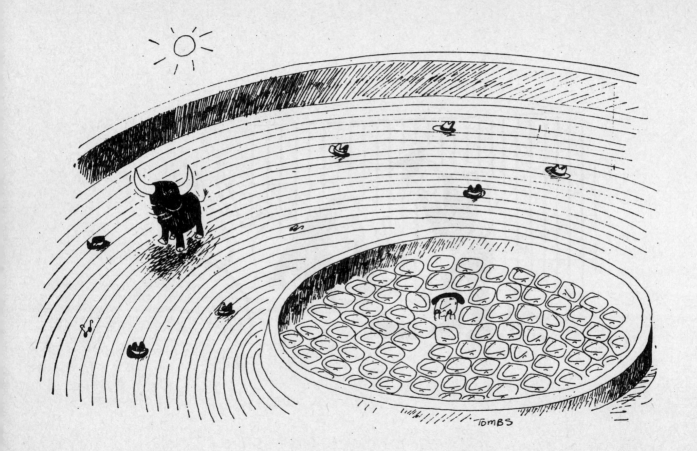

"At least as a rug you'd get near a fire occasionally."

"I'm sorry, sir – we don't do part exchange."

"I'm sorry, son, but it was kinder to put your lemming out of its misery."

"I hate it when he gets into one of his partying moods!"

"I eat what I like and then let the food
fight it out inside!"

"Never mind the delay – you've got your car cleaned."

"We're not really supposed to feed them."

"I think it's high time that dog was emptied."

"As far as I'm concerned he could stay out all night."

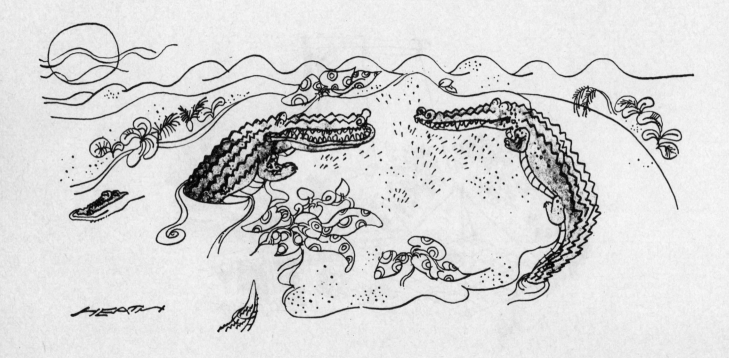

"I've bequeathed my body to Bond Street."

"And yet he's hopeless with people."

"...and two long range weather forecasters. That's the lot."